CHAMPIONS OF THE GREAT COMMISSION

Steel Valleys

CHAMPIONS OF THE GREAT COMMISSION

Steel Valleys

Shirley Carlson

Illustrations by
Loren Ullom

Adapted from
Another Valley, Another Victory, Another Love
by Valetta Steel Crumley
and
Mission Accomplished Under Sentence of Death
by Ed Erny

OMS - ONE MISSION SOCIETY

By God's grace, One Mission Society unites, inspires and equips Christians to make disciples of Jesus Christ, multiplying dynamic communities of believers around the world.

One Mission Society is an evangelical, interdenominational faith mission that makes disciples of Jesus Christ through intentional evangelism, planting churches and training national leaders in Africa, Asia, the Caribbean, Europe and Latin America. OMS then joins with those churches in global partnerships to reach the rest of the world.

One Mission Society
PO Box A
Greenwood, IN 46142
317.888.3333
www.onemissionsociety.org
www.onemissionkids.org

Steel Valleys
Copyright © 2011 by One Mission Society

ISBN 978-1-880338-01-8

Cover design by W. Foster Pilcher.

Printed in the United States of America by
Evangel Press, Nappanee, Indiana 46550

Thank you for your interest in our children's book series, *Champions of the Great Commission.* We at One Mission Society pray that this story will inspire you to share the love of Jesus with others as He calls us to do in Matthew 28:19–20: *"Therefore go and make disciples of all nations, baptizing them in the name of the Father and of the Son and of the Holy Spirit, and teaching them to obey everything I have commanded you. And surely I am with you always, to the very end of the age."* At the end of each chapter, you will find questions, prayers and Scripture that we hope will inspire you to follow Jesus daily.

CONTENTS

CHAPTER 1

VALETTA, A DYNAMIC GIRL

Valetta Stevenson straightened her bent, aching back and stretched as tall as her eight-year-old body could stretch. The sun shone down on her blond hair, producing beads of sweat that dripped down her forehead and onto her cheeks. If she stuck her tongue out at just the right time, she could taste the salty drops.

All afternoon, her dad had been digging the dry clods of dirt on their property to find potatoes. The four eldest children's job was to pick up the potatoes and break off the stubborn soil. Valetta hated the feeling of dirt on her hands, and now, she had had enough! Leaving her little pile of potatoes, she wandered off to lie down in the shade of the old barn across the field.

"Where do you think you're going, little lady?" she heard her dad say, kindly but firmly.

"Well, Dad, I've had enough for today. I want to do something more fun."

Her brothers, Eugene and Ronnie, couldn't believe their ears. "Oh, no, is she in for it!" they said, laughing as they pushed their forks into the ground.

"You can play when you've finished your section of ground, Valetta," her dad stated.

"But I really don't want to pick up another dirty potato," she responded, relaxing flat on her back with her legs twirling circles in the air.

All the children stopped their work and watched as their father walked over to a nearby tree. With his pocket knife, he began whittling a branch that looked like it would make a suitable switch. As quick as a flash, Valetta's feet hit the ground, and she scurried around like a squirrel, searching for wayward potatoes. Valetta respected her father, and she knew that if he disciplined her, she deserved it.

In 1940, when Valetta was seven, her father had moved his family to this 22-acre farm near Temperance, Michigan. He was good at carpentry, and he had added a room onto the farmhouse because of the growing number of kids. He even enclosed the back porch to make a guest room for Grandmother when she stayed with them.

Mr. Stevenson loved his wife and seven children, and he loved God. Each evening after supper, he read from the family Bible. Each child took a turn talking to God. Then, together, they prayed the Lord's Prayer.

Valetta loved the way her dad spoke with God, just like he was in a conversation with a friend. His friendship with God made her think about her own relationship with Him. She knew He heard her prayers, but she wanted to make sure she belonged to Him.

One day when she was 12, Valetta slipped to her knees on the cold linoleum floor in her room. She confessed to God every sin she could remember. She then asked Jesus to come into her life. She knew immediately that God answered her prayer. It wasn't because she heard voices or felt anything unusual; she just knew.

Valetta wanted to tell her mother that she was now a Christian, but she hesitated. Her mother didn't talk about God often, even though she loved Him. She wasn't the sort of person to wrap her arms around her children and say, "I love you." Valetta wished she could be closer to her mother.

Mrs. Stevenson worked hard, keeping up with the laundry and cooking for a family of nine. She knew how to save every spare penny and made sure the children each had a few sets of clothing. She also assigned tasks to the children as they prepared for school each morning.

Arthur, the eldest boy fed and milked the cow. Mrs. Stevenson cooked the oatmeal while Leonora and Valetta prepared the school lunches. Eugene and Ronnie dressed themselves and tied shoelaces for the younger ones, while little Sharon sat in the high chair, watching the busyness.

The constant demands from her family wore Valetta's mother out, and she didn't have much energy left to just be with her children.

When Valetta was 14, she longed to leave home. A youth choir from a Christian high school and college visited her local church. Valetta saw this as her opportunity to talk to her parents. She felt nervous and wondered what they would say, but she knew she must ask them.

"Dad, Mom. I've been thinking that I would love to leave home to attend high school." Valetta bit her lip and waited intently for her parents' reaction.

"We think that is something we could give our blessing to," her dad said.

Valetta couldn't believe it! "I can hardly wait," she told them.

11

SOMETHING TO THINK ABOUT

What would it have been like for Valetta's parents in the 1930s, raising a family of seven children? What priority did Valetta's father have for his children concerning their relationship with God?

_____

_____

_____

_____

ACTION PLAN

Write a letter to your parents or guardians, thanking them for caring for you. You may want to draw a picture of yourself with them.

_____

_____

_____

_____

VERSE TO MEMORIZE

Teach them (God's words) _to your children. Talk about them when you are at home and when you are on the road, when you are going to bed and when you are getting up again._
—Deuteronomy 11:19

TALK TO GOD

Thank God for your parents and the people He has used to teach you how to live. Ask Him to help you make the right choices and always put Him first.

MY PERSONAL DIARY

_____

_____

_____

_____

_____

CHAPTER 2

HENRY, A DIAMOND IN THE ROUGH

Mrs. Potsbury, the pastor's wife and Henry Steel's Sunday school teacher, was beside herself. What was she going to do with this infuriating youngster? At times, he drove her crazy, yet she couldn't keep herself from wrapping her arms around him in a great big hug.

"I'd be a Christian, Ma, if you'd convince me it's worthwhile," Henry teased her. (She wasn't his mother, but that was what he called her.) He really did want to know if he could trust God. He continued, "It hasn't got you very far, has it? A pitiful salary and a lifetime of broken-down pastors' homes? There's no future in being a Christian." He thought he had cornered the preacher's wife.

She calmly looked him in the eyes, and with a loving tone, she replied, "It may be hard, but Henry, I wouldn't change one bit of my life."

Mrs. Potsbury often buried her face in her hands and prayed for this young boy who craved so much affection. "God, would You do something in his life to bring him to You?" she wept. She would not give up loving Henry and praying for him. She

13

knew God had great plans for him. Henry was on this earth for a reason.

Henry was the youngest of four children. His mother died when he was six weeks old. Henry's father tried to care for the family on his own, but it was too hard for him. He sent baby Henry to live with his grandmother. She was a sweet lady who adored her grandson.

When Henry was in fifth grade, his father remarried and asked Henry to move back home. Home was a garage that had been converted to a temporary garage and was too small for the family. It wasn't built well, and it had no running water and no refrigerator. Even though his grandmother didn't have a lot, Henry was used to more personal space with her. She also treated him with kindness. Now, he had to adjust to a strict father and unpleasant living conditions.

Mr. Steel was a tough man, and he set many rules for his children. It was hard to live that way, not feeling loved by his father. But Henry looked up to his older brother Jim. When Jim joined the army, Henry was upset and desperately lonely. His father agreed to let him move back with his grandmother, who had rented the house next door. She moved there so that she could keep an eye on the children, especially Henry, who was like her own son.

Under his grandmother's care and Mrs. Potsbury's guidance, Henry began to thrive. He developed a sense of humor and showed that he could be a leader among his classmates. He joined the Boy Scouts and worked so hard at achieving his awards that his scout master said, "No one in the history of the Clio Scout troop has ever progressed this quickly!" Henry received a trophy which read, "The Best Scout in Troop 101."

Henry learned how to plant a half-acre garden, care for a dairy business and speak in front of groups of people. As he became good at public speaking and debate, God put an idea in his head. *If I ever give myself to God, I would like to preach!* he thought. But really, he wanted a job that paid more money.

"If the Lord wants you to preach, Henry," Mrs. Potsbury assured him, "He'll prove it to you by blessing your efforts."

When he was 17, Henry's older sister Catherine invited him to her graduation at Spring Arbor College. Henry felt uncomfortable in a huge room filled with many Christians. The speaker interrupted his thoughts, "I know we don't usually invite people to make a decision to follow Christ at a graduation ceremony," he said. Henry sat up and listened more intently. The speaker continued, "But I feel that God is speaking to someone here. Now, in front of this large group of people, will you come to meet God?"

Why was Henry struggling so much with making this decision? He knew that he should respond, but he couldn't force himself out of his chair.

As Henry was thinking, a young man placed his hand on his shoulder and said, "Somehow, I feel this is a very important moment for you. Choose God. You'll never be sorry." Henry stood up to leave the building. He was not going to do this Christian thing! But as he got to his feet to walk out of the building, he saw the altar at the front filled with young people just like him, responding to God's call.

Henry quickly walked in front of all those people to join the crowds on their knees. He didn't care who saw him. That day, he said yes to God. The Potsburys were filled with happiness. God had answered their sincere prayers. Their lost and lonely friend had found his security in God.

The first thing Henry knew he must do now that he was a Christian was to ask forgiveness from all the people he had offended. If he had taken anything from them, he would return it. He had to make things right.

Henry felt new desires growing inside him. Jesus wasn't some person in the Bible that people told stories about. He was real. Now, more than anything, Henry wanted to preach. Reverend Potsbury began teaching Henry how to study the Bible and how to prepare and preach sermons.

His first sermon was titled, "The Donkey Sermon." It was based on Luke 19:28–35, which tells of a time when Jesus needed to borrow a donkey. Henry thought about that: *Suppose the owners of the donkey had other plans for the animal?* Henry knew that he really was preaching to himself. God was the owner and he was the donkey, and God had other plans for him. Henry said in his sermon, "We may not want to go the way Jesus asks us to go. But He has asked, and that is enough."

Something to Think About

Why was Henry so disrespectful when he spoke to Mrs. Potsbury? Why do you think God's Holy Spirit prompted Mrs. Potsbury to pray often for Henry? Do you believe that God has people praying for you?

_____

_____

_____

_____

Action Plan

If you know of people who have prayed for you over the years, write a special letter or card to them. Thank them for their faithfulness in praying that you would give your life to Jesus.

_____

_____

_____

_____

Verse to Memorize

This means that anyone who belongs to Christ has become a new person. The old life is gone; a new life has begun!
—2 Corinthians 5:17

Talk to God

God created you, and He sent His Son Jesus to die for you. He would have done that whether or not you decide to follow Jesus. Thank God now for loving you more than anything in the world. Ask Him to help you love Him more each day.

My Personal Diary

_____

_____

_____

_____

_____

CHAPTER 3

THE DREAM TEAM

Henry Steel had no money, but he knew that college was next in God's plan for him. He was thrilled when he got a chance to earn money to help pay for school. The Free Methodist Church offered a one-year college scholarship for the person who sold the most subscriptions for their youth magazine. Henry took the challenge seriously.

He contacted the church leaders in the surrounding towns. He asked if they would buy subscriptions for the small churches that could not afford to pay for their own. Henry worked hard to convince people that they needed the magazine.

Near the end of August, Henry received an official-looking letter. It read, "We are pleased to inform you that you have won the national contest." Henry was thrilled. He began packing immediately to go to Spring Arbor College.

Henry didn't know that his closest competitor had been a young, pretty girl named Valetta Stevenson. Valetta had come in second place in the competition. She just missed out on receiving the financial help she also needed.

"I'm glad you won the scholarship, Henry," Valetta congratulated him as she shook his hand when they met after the competition. "Well ... well, thank you, Miss Stevenson," he managed to stutter. He had noticed this girl and couldn't get her out of his mind. He couldn't believe he was actually talking to her now. He had heard about her devotion to God and her good school work. He wanted to get to know the person under that beautiful blond hair.

God also seemed to be preparing Valetta for Henry. He was a bit loud and awkward, but his self-confidence reminded Valetta of her dad. Henry and Valetta found in each other the love and security they both needed. God was the glue that held them together.

After Henry graduated from junior college, he and Valetta were married on July 7, 1951, three years after they met. Without a house, a job or savings, they moved into a mobile home in Valetta's home town of Temperance, Michigan. Henry began working at a car factory, as well as with his father-in-law. He also worked part time as a youth pastor at Valetta's home church with Pastor Larry Burr. Valetta found a job as a secretary.

Within one year, two exciting things happened. First, they found out they were going to have a baby. Then, a small church 100 miles away in Sherwood, Michigan, asked Henry to be their pastor. God had blessed Henry and Valetta with a place to live and work. But how would they know if it really was God leading them to this church? In the past, the town had factories, a high school, a college and a railway station. Now, all those things were gone. Why would they go to an old church, where few people attended on Sundays? It would probably close anyway, due to lack of interest.

This offer came at an interesting time. Henry had been accepted recently to a college in New York. The couple

19

already had plans to travel soon after the baby was born. Then, suddenly, he received this invitation to become a pastor. Henry could put into practice the skills to be a minister that he had learned over the past few years.

Henry and Valetta had their plan made; changing it now would be unsettling. No, he didn't want to take the position. He wanted more education. But, he did agree to preach at the little country church for a few Sundays until they could find someone else. In the meantime, he would pray about the offer. However, he didn't plan to accept it.

On the first Sunday that Henry was to preach, he dutifully drove the 100 miles to the small country church. To everyone's surprise, some young people had heard that a young preacher was coming, and they were already waiting inside when the preacher arrived.

The weeks passed. Henry had been counting off the Sundays that he had committed to preach. But God was doing something to change his mind. When the young pastor saw the youth and their excitement, he felt energized. He wanted to get to know them better and help them in their spiritual growth. He understood a little of what Jesus felt in Matthew 9:36 when he saw the crowds and felt compassion for them.

God was speaking to him from his first sermon. God had plans for the donkey that were different than the owner's plans. God had a different idea for Henry and Valetta also. Instead of heading back to college, God wanted them to shepherd this little church. Their "no" turned to a "yes," and they knew immediately that they had made the right decision.

"Rev. Cutler," Henry said as he spoke over the phone, "you can stop looking for a pastor for Sherwood. The Lord has shown me that it's the place for us right now."

"Well, Henry," the church superintendent said, chuckling, "I knew that you would say yes. So I never even looked for anyone else for the job!"

Little Daniel Phillip Steel was born on September 2, 1952. Ten days later, Henry and Valetta moved to Sherwood. Henry quickly learned how to be a daddy and how to care for a church. He put all of his energy into both tasks. He wanted to do the best job he could for God, for Valetta and for the people of Sherwood. He knew that God had brought Valetta into his life to help him become the man God intended him to be.

The young family's arrival woke up the sleepy little town. Henry dove into his new job with excitement. One of the first things he did was visit the homes in the community so that each person could meet the new pastor. Sometimes people have wrong ideas about others until they meet face to face. Once people met Henry, though, they wanted to be his friend. People who hadn't been to church in years began attending because they had met a man who would teach them about God.

About 25 people usually attended Sunday services at the church before the Steels arrived. Soon, 50 were there, and before long, the ushers had to find seats for 150! Henry and Valetta invited the young people to their home for meals and Bible studies. They trained Sunday school teachers, organized Bible quizzes and thought about how they could include the talents of each person in the church.

To get involved in the community, Henry volunteered as a fireman and wrote short sermons for the local newspaper. He even bought a second-hand printing press to print and distribute Christian messages and notices about church events.

So many people attended Sunday services now that the little church building couldn't hold them all! After the Steels had ministered in Sherwood for just two years, the church had already outgrown their building.

Pastor Henry suggested to the people that they pay $1,000 for the empty church building across the street. Fixing it up would cost about $6,000. Henry made a picture of a huge thermometer to record how much money was raised for the "Build for Tomorrow" project. As the money came in, the red line on the thermometer went higher.

People came from everywhere to help. Volunteers painted, hammered, washed windows, scrubbed floors and pulled weeds. Some of the women who liked to cook made meals, and Valetta's father, who was good at carpentry, rebuilt the steeple.

Valetta and Henry were so busy and happy. They were surprised when they discovered that God was blessing them with another baby! Leon Henry was born on October 19, 1954—a little brother for two-year-old Danny.

SOMETHING TO THINK ABOUT

Why does God want Christians to worship with other Christians? How is a pastor like a shepherd?

_____

_____

_____

_____

ACTION PLAN

Think of someone you know who may not know God, and invite him to go to church or youth group with you. Who will you invite?

_____

_____

_____

_____

VERSE TO MEMORIZE

Seek the Kingdom of God above all else, and live righteously, and he will give you everything you need. —Matthew 6:33

TALK TO GOD

God wants to help you grow in your faith in Him. He wants to be your shepherd. Ask Him to change your life and make you into the person He created you to be.

MY PERSONAL DIARY

_____

_____

_____

_____

_____

CHAPTER 4

DANNY, THE TOWN'S BOY

"Hi ya, Mr. Frank," Danny greeted as he strolled down the main street.

"Hi, ya, Danny. How's the Lone Ranger doing this morning?"

Two-year-old Danny strutted hand in hand with his daddy, cowboy hat covering his blond hair and pair of toy guns hanging from his holster. Danny was a popular little boy around the small town. Each day, the father and son team chatted with the people in town as they made their way to the post office to collect their mail. Little Danny looked up at each person with his big blue eyes and melted their hearts with his wide grin and ready conversation.

As well as pastoring the little Free Methodist church in Sherwood, Henry often preached out of town. One of those times, Valetta took baby Leon and little Danny to visit their grandparents. After the visit, Valetta noticed that Danny seemed cranky and irritable. He wasn't his usual cheerful self and seemed close to tears for no obvious reason. She told herself that he was just unsettled from the traveling and the change of routine.

One morning, as Valetta finish washing dishes, she looked out the kitchen window. She noticed Danny struggling to get his tricycle handlebars exactly where he wanted them.

"Mommy, my arm hurts," he complained as he looked up to meet his mother's glance. Valetta dropped her dish rag and ran out the back, letting the screen door slam. Danny was more distressed than she expected.

"I'll help you, little guy," she said as she scooped her son up in her arms. "Let's go visit the doctor. He'll make you feel better."

After examining Danny, the doctor looked concerned. Valetta felt very uncomfortable. "Mrs. Steel," he said, "I think there may be something wrong with Danny's bone. If you will take him to the hospital tomorrow, we'll do a few more tests."

At the hospital the next day, the doctor had bad news. Instead of finding a bruise or something that could be fixed easily, he found a much bigger problem. "I'm afraid," the doctor began, as he spoke seriously to Henry and Valetta, "your little Danny has something called leukemia. It is cancer of the blood."

Henry and Valetta had heard of leukemia, but they never thought it would affect their family. Why did this happen? How did Danny get it? Surely the doctor could give some pills to fix it so they could all go home and Danny's arm would stop hurting.

"There isn't a cure for it," the doctor's voice broke into their thoughts. "With certain medicines, Danny might live another six months."

"Six months!" Henry exclaimed. "This can't be real." Henry clasped Valetta's hand with a tightness that matched the tightness of her throat. She could hardly breathe. What were these words she was hearing about her perfect little boy?

"Are you sure?" Henry asked, hoping for any good news that would give them some hope.

"I'm sorry," the doctor managed to say, "This is the hardest news I've ever given anyone."

Henry and Valetta took their little boy home to care for him. During the next five months, they regularly took Danny to the hospital, where he received medical care. He didn't feel well and began to look sick. He didn't have the energy to play with Leon, his baby brother who had joined the family a few months earlier. And often, he didn't feel like eating. Sometimes, when he did feel well enough, his mommy would strap his toy gun belt on him, and wearing his big cowboy hat, he would go outside and have fun with his daddy.

Valetta cried and prayed often during those days when Danny was sick. She wanted to be with him as much as she could because she knew that he wouldn't live to celebrate his third birthday. She lay with him on the bed and read stories to him when he was too weak to sit up. She rocked him in her arms through the night hours when his fevers wouldn't go away. She sang soothing songs to him when he cried in pain and confusion.

"Jesus loves me this I know, for the Bible tells me so," she sang as she held his frail, little body close to hers. "Little ones to Him belong; they are weak but He is strong."

One morning, Danny didn't wake up. He had gone to be with Jesus. The thin little body lay in the bed, but the real Danny, the wide-smiled, cheerful little boy who made a friend of everyone, had gone to be with his best friend of all, his heavenly Father.

SOMETHING TO THINK ABOUT
Why do you think God allows some people to get sick and die? God's son, Jesus, died on the cross for you and me. What do you think that was like for God?

_____

_____

_____

_____

ACTION PLAN
Think of someone who is not feeling well or has had a family member die. Make a card to send them, and write a little note to let them know you care.

_____

_____

_____

_____

VERSE TO MEMORIZE
"Unless you accept God's kingdom in the simplicity of a child, you'll never get in." Then, gathering the children up in his arms, he laid his hands of blessing on them. —Mark 10:14-15 (The Message)

TALK TO GOD
Pray for your friends who are sick or sad. Ask God to give them the courage they need to live through each day. Ask Him to show Himself to them so they don't feel alone or afraid.

MY PERSONAL DIARY

_____

_____

_____

_____

_____

CHAPTER 5

CHUCK, LARRY AND FRANK

Chuck stood at the home plate, bat poised over his shoulder, ready to strike. "Come on now, Chuck," Henry cheered. "Hit that ball over the fence!" The curve ball zoomed past Chuck so fast he didn't stand a chance of hitting it.

"Strike three!" yelled the umpire. Chuck dropped the bat and walked off the field, kicking the dirt with his foot.

"Good try, Chuck," Henry encouraged. "You gave it all you had!" Henry threw his arm around the teen's shoulder, and together, they headed home.

Chuck was one of the boys in Henry's first Sunday school class, which he led just after he graduated from high school. He wanted all of the kids to know that Jesus loved them and died for them.

Henry didn't only go to their ball games; he also went hiking and fishing and found ways to just hang out with the guys. He wanted to be an example of a man who loved God and lived out his faith. Some of the fathers of these boys didn't know Jesus, so if Henry didn't show them what a true Christian man was, who would?

Chuck remembered one time when he was fishing out on the lake with Henry and Henry encouraged him about his future. "Chuck," he said with an air of confidence, "God has great plans for you. He will make them happen if you stay faithful to Him." Those were just the words Chuck needed to hear.

After Henry had graduated from Spring Arbor College and married Valetta, Pastor Larry Burr invited Henry to work with him each weekend at his church in Temperance. Henry already knew Pastor Larry's brother, Harry, who had been Henry's friend throughout his college years. Valetta's parents also attended the church in Temperance. Her dad thought that Henry would be a great student pastor. He could learn a lot from Pastor Larry.

Just as Henry had been a role model for the boys in his Sunday school class, now Pastor Larry took Henry under his wing to show him what it meant to be a pastor. Henry would have to stay close to God and care for his wife and children. He would also have to study the Bible, pray to God, teach and preach. He was responsible before God to care for the spiritual growth of the people in his town.

Larry Burr was serious about being a good role model for Henry. He wanted to teach the young pastor many things that he had learned over the years. Larry wanted to use what God had already taught him to help Henry avoid making mistakes like he had made. Henry watched his mentor closely and began to catch his excitement about reaching the world for Jesus. Years later, when Henry was asked to describe the most "interesting person" he had ever met, he wrote about Pastor Larry.

I want to talk about my friend, Lawrence E. Burr ... He began working as the pastor of a small, struggling church that needed a lot of help. In six years, he made it into a healthy and fabulous church ... I have watched how Mr. Burr responds when God has blessed him and also in the times when he feels like he has failed. No matter what hard times life threw at him, he was full of energy and excitement about what God was doing, even when he couldn't yet see it.

Because of Larry's excellent training, the same words would one day describe Henry Steel.

Henry took his job as senior pastor at the church in Sherwood very seriously. He had learned to be thorough in everything, and he visited many homes in that little town. One man he met was Frank. Because of Henry's friendship and persistence, Frank changed the way he lived his life.

Frank was much like Henry had been before he knew Jesus. On the outside, Frank appeared confident and sure of himself. But on the inside, he was insecure and didn't feel good about himself. When they first met, Frank thought that he had to give Henry excuses about why he didn't attend church. Henry didn't mind. He just wanted to be Frank's friend and show him Jesus' love, even if Frank never went to church. That's what Jesus would have done.

Instead of pushing Frank to go to church on Sundays, Henry asked his new friend, "Frank, you know this area well. Can you suggest some good places a man can go hunting?" Frank was surprised. Here was the new pastor in town asking him to go hunting instead of making him sit in a church pew!

The two men often went hunting together. As they began to trust and respect each other more, Frank saw what a real Christian was through his pastor friend. He even attended church sometimes. Henry knew that making a choice to follow Jesus takes time. His responsibility was to be a friend to Frank, not to judge him, especially when he made bad choices in his life.

Frank had not decided to give his life to Jesus yet. He still wanted to live his life the way *he* wanted, whether it pleased

God or not. He still spent time with people that chose to make poor decisions. One night, around Halloween, Frank and his friends wanted to crash a party at the church. They were rude, interrupted people's conversations and made a lot of noise. However, they were surprised when the Christians at the church didn't get upset or angry. Instead, they welcomed the intruders and treated them with love and respect. Frank was caught off guard. He didn't know how to respond to being treated well when he and his friends were being so disrespectful and impolite.

"Come on guys," Frank said as he grabbed his friends to leave. "Let's get out of here."

Henry saw what happened that night, but he kept hunting and talking with Frank. He knew that Jesus is the Good Shepherd who doesn't give up looking for even one lost sheep. Frank was that lost sheep, and Henry wanted to help Frank come to Jesus.

As time went on, Henry began to tell his friend about how he had become a Christian. Frank listened carefully to what Henry said. He even said later about Henry, *I have often thought back about how Henry became a Christian. The way he lived every day proved to me that he was real and not faking about his relationship with God. Because he lived what he spoke about, I knew that I wanted to know God like he did.*

One afternoon as Henry and Frank sat on the front porch chatting, Frank blurted out, "I want to become a Christian, but I don't know what to do. Do I have to get on my knees or go to the altar at the front of the church?"

"No, you don't have to do that," Henry responded to Frank's honest question. "God hears us wherever we are. But if you make your private decision to follow Christ public, then you might encourage other people who haven't yet decided to come to Jesus."

Henry couldn't wait for Sunday. During the morning service, Frank thought a lot about the decision he was going to make. At the evening service, he got up from his seat, boldly

31

walked to the altar and humbly knelt before God. He wasn't thinking about people watching him. He just wanted to publicly confirm that God accepted him as His child and that the Holy Spirit was changing him from the inside out.

Frank's life changed. He had a new desire to know God better and serve Him. God had brought this lost sheep home.

SOMETHING TO THINK ABOUT

Do you know someone that loves God and would be willing to spend time with you, teaching you more about God? That person could be a role model for you. Do you know someone that you would like to spend time with? You could be a good example for that person of how a Christian lives.

_____

_____

_____

_____

ACTION PLAN

Who can you be a good friend to? What can you do to spend some quality time with that person?

_____

_____

_____

_____

VERSE TO MEMORIZE

You have heard me teach things that have been confirmed by many reliable witnesses. Now teach these truths to trustworthy people who will be able to pass them on to others. —2 Timothy 2:2

TALK TO GOD

Jesus spent time teaching 12 disciples when He was on earth. Ask God to bring someone into your life who can teach you more about Him. Pray also that He will bring someone into your life to whom you can be a good example.

MY PERSONAL DIARY

_____

_____

_____

_____

CHAPTER 6

ANOTHER ILLNESS

By 1957, Henry and his family had moved to Kalamazoo, Michigan, to lead a different church. One morning, Henry coughed a deep cough as he headed to the bathroom for his morning shave. He thought about all of the work he needed to do. He loved his work as a minister. He got to study the Bible and preach what God showed him. He loved being with people, and he always had someone to talk with or listen to. He prayed with people who were sick or hurting or having problems.

Most of all, he loved his family, especially his beautiful wife Valetta, who helped him so much. He could never be the person he had become without her. He adored his son, Leon, and daughter, Lorna, who was born the year after Danny died. He still felt sad that Danny was no longer with them. But he looked forward to heaven where they would be together again.

He lathered his face with good-smelling soap and began winding the razor around the familiar shape of his cheeks. He could do this blindfolded. He'd been shaving for 10 years and had the time it took down to just a few minutes. But this day, as he pulled his head up, chin protruding to get those stubborn neck hairs, he stopped his routine. Puzzled, he saw that one side of his neck was bigger than the other. What was that about?

"Valetta," he called, "come and look at this."

"That's unusual," Valetta said. "Maybe we should stop by the doctor's office and ask him to take a look at it."

Now that he thought about it, his left arm had felt a little strange the past few weeks. He especially felt it when he turned the steering wheel on the car. Maybe he'd pulled a muscle in a ball game. *No big deal,* he thought, but he agreed that he should see the doctor just in case it was something more serious.

The doctor wasn't too alarmed. He prescribed antibiotics, but that didn't seem to change the lump. So several days later, the doctor tested a small piece of the tissue. That test didn't show anything out of the ordinary. During the cold winter months, the swelling increased, so Henry made an appointment with a specialist at a big hospital.

"You sure do look funny in that skimpy gown," Valetta joked when she went to Henry's room after the doctors had seen him. "Valetta, my dear," Henry said in a rather serious tone, ignoring her funny comment. "I want you to sit down."

Valetta's stomach turned into a knot. She didn't like the tone of her husband's voice. "Valetta," Henry continued, "the lump in my neck is Hodgkin's disease."

Valetta's quizzical look prompted Henry to continue. "Hodgkin's disease is cancer of the lymph nodes. They can give me medicines to help me feel better for a while. The bad thing is that they don't have medicines that will make the cancer go away totally, so I will die from it eventually. But the specialist told me that I still have several years to live."

Henry's words seemed like a mumbled voice in the background as Valetta tried to understand what he said. She had not heard anything else her husband said after he mentioned the word cancer. Fresh memories of little Danny flooded into her mind. Cancer: what a terrible thing. What was Henry saying? That now he had cancer?

"What did you say?" Valetta said as she tried to gather her thoughts, "The lump is cancer?"

"Yes, my dear," Henry said as he held her hands firmly in his. "Don't be alarmed, honey, because there is a lot of hope. God is on our side."

"But, you've never been sick," Valetta stammered, as she pulled away from him. "You're only 26!"

"We may have as long as two years, maybe more," Henry said, as much to himself as to his wife. "I want to spend that time doing something that will last beyond my own lifetime. I want you to help me think about how we will do that."

The next few weeks were like living in a bad dream. It was hard to concentrate on doing the daily tasks. However, Henry and Valetta shared some very special conversations together as they talked about how they would spend Henry's remaining time on earth.

Larry Burr, Henry's mentor and pastor from the Temperance church, shared some things that were timely and significant for the Steel family as they made decisions. Larry had stopped working as a pastor in the church and joined a mission organization called OMS International (now One Mission Society). The two men sat in the hospital room, chatting late into the night. As they talked, Henry felt more and more that he should share Jesus with people beyond his own town, even outside the United States, into other countries.

After their conversation, Henry asked, "Larry, do you think God might have a place for me in missions?"

"Henry," Larry answered seriously, "if God has put that desire in your heart, I have no doubt that He is preparing you for a future in missionary work. If you feel strong enough, take a trip to the mission field," Larry suggested. "Preach to those who have never heard, and you may eventually see their faces in eternity."

Before Henry could go anywhere to preach about Jesus, he had to have some medical treatments that made him feel tired and sick. He didn't feel like eating very much. He could only lie in bed and rest while the bad cancer cells in his body were attacked by strong radiation treatments.

Henry asked the church leaders to pray and anoint him with oil, just like the Bible instructs. They trusted God to heal him, and they waited for His answer. Henry knew that God can easily heal someone of a disease that has no cure. But he also knew that sometimes He chooses not to.

For the next year, Henry pastored at the Kalamazoo church. After he received the treatments, the cancer went into remission, which means the cancer cells were not active and his body felt almost normal again. But remission is usually temporary, which was the case with Henry. The cancer became active again, so Henry continued to receive regular radiation treatments. When he did, he couldn't do his usual work. After a few weeks, when his body recovered from the harsh treatments, he was back to preaching and visiting people in his congregation.

Valetta noticed that her husband's sermons sounded different. He began speaking about things such as sharing Jesus with a neighbor, being kind and loving people who are difficult to love. There was no time to waste on unimportant things. He wanted to fill his days with as much good as he could before he went to heaven to be with Jesus and his baby, Danny.

When Henry was feeling a little better after one of his radiation treatments, he attended a missions conference and chatted with an OMS missionary named Bill Gillam. After their talk, Henry was convinced that God wanted him to join OMS and work with them for the last years of his life.

However, he still had work to complete at the Kalamazoo church, like finishing the new church building and buying buses to transport more children to Sunday school.

He decided to work at the Kalamazoo church for the next year. Then he would go on a mission trip to South America before starting work with the mission. If he was going to learn how to share about missions, he wanted to visit one of the countries where the missionaries worked.

As Henry finished his work at the church, he began preparing for his trip. More than a year had passed, and there was no sign of cancer in his body. Maybe God had healed him after all. Healing or no healing, he still believed God wanted him to work in missions.

But packing his bag one morning, Henry felt a strangely familiar feeling. His body felt like it was on fire. He knew that the cancer had returned.

SOMETHING TO THINK ABOUT

When Henry found out he had cancer, he said, "I want to spend that time doing something that will last beyond my own lifetime." What do you think about those words? What if you didn't have much time left on earth? How would you spend your days?

_____

_____

_____

_____

ACTION PLAN

Write down some ideas of what you want to accomplish in life.

_____

_____

_____

_____

VERSE TO MEMORIZE

Teach us to realize how short our lives are. Then our hearts will become wise. —Psalm 90:12 (NIrV)

TALK TO GOD

We know that this earth is a place where we live only for a short time. Heaven is our real home. Ask God to show you what He wants you to do with your life.

MY PERSONAL DIARY

_____

_____

_____

_____

_____

CHAPTER 7

A DYING MAN SPEAKS TO DYING MEN

Henry lay on the uncomfortable hospital bed, tolerating the radiation treatment that made him sick. He decided that he would go ahead with his trip to Ecuador and Colombia in a few days. So, Valetta and the little ones went to stay with her parents, and Henry, with a bottle of pain medication, boarded the airplane, feeling weak and nauseated.

Henry flew to Ecuador first, where he talked with Bible school students. He felt energized by their desire to study and learn about God. Missionary Stewart Sparrow described Henry's activity: *Despite the language barrier, Henry got along great with the people of Guayaquil. They knew that he loved them.* Henry even ruined his good trousers playing basketball with them one afternoon, but he didn't mind. He knew that people were more important than clothes.

Henry traveled with Bill Douce, the mission doctor, through the city of Cuenca. They also went 12,000 feet above sea level to visit the isolated Saraguro Indians. Henry felt chilled to the bone with the cold weather. His stomach was upset, and the rough and winding road made him feel sick. He chose not to feel sorry for himself though. Instead, he thought about the less-than-perfect conditions the missionaries had to live with every day.

Dr. Bill informed Henry that the Saraguros had threatened the missionaries many times and warned them to leave the area. But the missionaries wanted to serve God, even if it was difficult. As the jeep made its way along the rough road, the seven passengers, cramped between supplies, prayed to God, "Father of all creation, You have led us to the Saraguro people. We trust You to protect us from those who want to hurt us." Henry knew that the doctor and his family and the two nurses lived in danger all the time.

Not long before Henry's visit to the Saraguros, five young missionary men had been killed when they tried to reach out to a primitive Indian group called the Aucas. Henry visited the HCJB mission radio station in the Andes Mountains where the men had worked. He felt honored to meet Marj Saint, the wife of Nate Saint, one of the men who had been killed. Although their lives ended tragically, God was at work in the hearts of the people they went to take the Gospel to.

Like the Aucas, the Saraguros had never met a missionary before. This was their first chance to hear about Jesus dying on the cross to bring them into a relationship with God.

The impact of what had happened to those missionaries touched Henry's heart. Henry wrote a letter to Valetta while flying low over dangerous mountain territory. He knew how much he depended on God for his safety. *I just realized today,* he wrote, *that a missionary has to trust God with his life, not just once, but every day.* Henry knew that God wanted the same commitment from him as well.

Henry flew from Ecuador to Medellín, Colombia, where he spoke at a Colombian pastor's conference. Most of the people

at the conference had been treated badly or imprisoned because of their love for Jesus.

In Cristalina, Colombia, he visited a 200-acre farm that OMS missionaries supervised. Colombians could live there, studying the Bible in the mornings and working on the farm in the afternoons. The farm produced watermelons and raised chickens, and the residents learned skills to earn a living. Henry also traveled on the river boat that missionaries used to take the message of Jesus to people that had never heard about Him.

Henry wrote to Valetta one morning, describing his early morning wake-up call. *I heard these sounds: a two-toned bell, a donkey braying, a dog barking, men talking and a jukebox blaring—all at 5:30 a.m.*

Henry experienced many new things during his two-month visit. He traveled in crowded vehicles over dirty, dusty roads. He trudged through mud, waded in streams and paddled through water in dugout canoes. He preached in churches the missionaries had started. He thanked God for the opportunity to travel and work with the missionaries.

When he returned home, Henry was excited about promoting missions wherever and however he could. As planned, he moved his family from Kalamazoo to Portland, Oregon, where he began working for the Mission. Henry traveled around Washington, Oregon, Idaho, Wyoming and Montana, telling people and churches about the work of OMS. He arranged meetings for missionaries. He also spoke of the need for missionaries to travel to the farthest parts of the world to tell people about Jesus.

Henry told about God's desire for His followers to share His love with a world of lost people. He preached a sermon titled *A Dying Man Speaks to Dying Men.* Henry was a living example of his sermon: "We are all going to die. My physical death is going to be very soon. Are we ready to die and meet God? Have we accepted Jesus' offer to enter heaven and have a relationship with God because of Jesus' death and resurrection?"

As Valetta watched her husband busy about his activities, she did all she could to make his life easier. She described his focused days as *priceless days, like the last and best perfume in a bottle that Henry determined to pour out upon his Savior.*

Something to Think About

Henry shared this in his sermon, *A Dying Man Speaks to Dying Men:* "There's no difference, really, between you and me, except for maybe a few years. For all of us, when we stand before Christ, it will not be a matter of how old we are or of what age we died, but of what we did with Jesus Christ." What does this quote mean to you?

_____
_____
_____
_____

Action Plan

Write to a missionary and ask how you can best pray for him or her.

_____
_____
_____
_____

Verse to Memorize

And I trust that my life will bring honor to Christ, whether I live or die. For to me, living means living for Christ, and dying is even better. —Philippians 1:21

Talk to God

No one knows how many years God will give us on this earth. But we do know that He wants us to live them wisely. Ask God how He wants you to tell others about Jesus and His love.

My Personal Diary

_____
_____
_____
_____
_____

CHAPTER 8

JOURNEY AROUND THE WORLD

"Valetta," Henry said over the phone, "how would you like to take a trip with me around the world?"

"You're kidding!" Valetta couldn't believe Henry was asking her this!

"No, really, someone is writing a blank check for both of us. I feel that God wants us to visit some of the countries where OMS works."

"But Henry," Valetta responded realistically, "what about Leon and Lorna and, well, you know, your health?"

"I know, dear," he replied, "but I think that we should make a list of all the obstacles and pray about each one specifically. Then, we can see what God will do."

"Well, when you put it like that," Valetta agreed, "I would love to go with you. Let's trust God for some miracles."

As Valetta and Henry prayed, God dealt with each request. Friends of the family offered to let the children stay with them. Then there was the bigger concern. Henry was again in remission, but he never knew how long it would last. What would the doctor say about such a venture?

"You're a very sick man," he reminded Henry. "But, if problems develop, you can always fly home." So with the itinerary planned and tickets in hand, Henry and Valetta boarded the plane for their first stop—Greece.

As the couple found their seats and fastened their seat belts, they held hands and prayed, "Heavenly Father, thank You for allowing us the privilege of making this trip to visit the places where You are working through OMS. Show us how to help people know You better. Thank You. In Jesus' name, Amen."

They arrived in Athens on Sunday, and Henry did what he normally did Sunday mornings—he preached. That evening, however, he began to feel more and more uncomfortable. His cough became worse, his stomach was upset, and he had a high fever. After seeing a doctor, Henry soon found himself in a foreign hospital, listening to the staff speak in a language he didn't understand.

Valetta found a Greek/English dictionary and wandered the markets at night, trying to find food her husband would like. Her mind was busy thinking, *Why did we come? What sort of a foolish decision was this when Henry is so ill?* But a couple of days after his treatment in the hospital, Henry was discharged. Though weak and not completely better, he and Valetta continued their travel plans.

In Acts 16–18, the apostle Paul preached to the Greeks. Henry's one wish in Athens was to stand on Mars Hill where Paul preached. After lots of huffing and puffing and stopping for rests, Valetta and their missionary friends helped Henry to the top of the hill. Together, they looked down at the city—a city lost without God. Henry's wish was fulfilled.

No experience as Christian workers in the United States could have prepared the Steels for the primitive sights in India. Missionary Wesley Duewel showed them around Allahabad and Benares, where he taught about God's Son. They watched as poor peasants as well as wealthy, educated Indians washed themselves in the dirty Ganges River, hoping to get rid of their sins. They didn't know that only Jesus could clean them from sin.

Mr. Duewel said that some of the Indian people had given their lives to Jesus. And they had even started telling others about Him as well. But those who did not trust in Jesus, even some from their own families, were doing bad things to hurt them because of their faith in Jesus. It wasn't easy being a Christian in India.

Henry and Valetta learned that in India the cow is considered a sacred animal and can't be hurt or used for food. They also learned that most Indians are Hindu and worship more than a million gods in the many temples and shrines scattered around the country.

Henry spoke to the students at the Allahabad Seminary. Their faces shone with the joy of Christ. Their expressions were such a contrast to those of the Indians that bathed in the dirty river.

Japan didn't seem as dark as India. The Japanese call their country "the land of the sun." Japanese worship many gods at their Shinto shrines.

Traveling to Tokyo, Henry felt very weak. He had dark circles below his eyes. Each breath was difficult to take, and he knew that it was only because of God's strength that he and Valetta had been able to fulfill all their traveling plans up to this point. But Henry was sad that he couldn't take part in the ceremony to lay a cornerstone in the new seminary building.

In Hong Kong, missionary Dale McClain took the Steels to places where OMS helped Chinese refugees. They had built schools on the top of high-rise apartments. In those buildings, the children attended school through the week and church on Sundays.

❖ ❖ ❖

When the Steels arrived at the Seoul airport, dozens of Korean Christians greeted them like royalty. The Koreans told Henry and Valetta, "We have prayed for you as you have traveled around the world on your journey. We believe God is going to visit us through you." The couple, both honored and humbled, was filled with a new burst of life.

Henry felt overwhelmed that God could use him, especially since he was so weak and sick. His pain worsened, and he couldn't stop coughing. But he refused to go to the hospital, despite the doctors' urging. Instead, Henry thought of the 500 pastors who had gathered together for meetings to hear him preach from the Bible. That's why he had come to this country. He didn't want to miss this opportunity, even if it meant that he would die at the pulpit.

In spite of his cancer, Henry did preach. God spoke through him to many Korean Christians about loving each other and not fighting with one another. Many Koreans didn't know about Jesus yet, so the Christians in Korea needed to concentrate on reaching their countrymen. They were thankful that Henry had spoken God's words to them.

One evening, late at night, Valetta couldn't sleep. She listened to her husband struggling to breathe. She opened her Bible to find strength from God's Word and read Isaiah 58:8, "Then your salvation will come like the dawn, and your wounds will quickly heal. Your godliness will lead you forward, and the glory of the Lord will protect you from behind."

"Lord," Valetta whispered, "what does this mean? Are You going to heal Henry in a different way than I want?"

"Soon," Valetta heard God speak to her, "I will take Henry to live with Me, and he will be healed totally."

Valetta knew then that her husband would die soon. Instead of living on earth with his sick body, he would join their baby Danny and many others in heaven. She was very sad, but her tears somehow brought comfort. One day, God would take away the pain.

With the energy that God gave, the Steels flew to Taiwan. OMS missionaries Rollie and Mildred Rice were waiting for Henry and Valetta to arrive. Valetta made Henry comfortable on the sofa, with a blanket tucked securely around his thinning body. He only had energy now to chat for a few minutes before he needed to rest and catch his breath. Together, they drank Chinese tea.

After Henry regained some energy, the group visited some Taiwanese churches and saw the beautiful Moon Lake.

The Steels had arrived in the city by train, so they had to return the same way. As they said goodbye to those who gathered at the station, Henry managed to say, "If I don't see you again here, I'll see you in heaven. Fair enough?" The train moved away from the platform out of sight as Henry clasped his hands above his head as a sign of victory.

In Hawaii, Valetta and Henry slept and relaxed. Henry could barely dress himself. His body was wearing out quickly, and he wondered how much longer he could keep going. Even though it was Valetta's 30th birthday, they didn't have the energy to go out and celebrate. Instead, they chose to drink a milkshake together across the street from the hotel. They enjoyed recalling the 12 years of marriage they had shared.

The plane screeched onto the runway in Los Angeles as they returned home. Henry and Valetta bowed in prayer, thanking God for the incredible way He had cared for them the past weeks. They couldn't contain their relief when they finally held their children in their arms. The family caught up on all the hugs and kisses they had missed. They laughed and cried and talked about all the adventures each person had while they were apart. After several days of relaxing, Valetta packed Henry's bag for the last time. The doctors were waiting for him at the hospital. Henry didn't feel like he could muster up the strength to even stand.

"Daddy, why are you always sick?" six-year-old Lorna asked as Henry was helped into the car.

"Sweetie," her father gently responded as he held her close, "Daddy has been sick since you were a baby. But we must thank Jesus that He has let me live long enough so that you can remember me." Henry didn't let go of his little girl. Leon watched with sad eyes, listening to his dad's final words. That would be the last time the children would see their daddy until they joined him in heaven.

Henry died a few days later. He left his weak and sick body behind to meet his Master in heaven.

For most of his short life, eight-year-old Leon had watched his father struggle with cancer. He knew now that his father's suffering had ended. As the family left the cemetery after Henry's funeral, Leon turned to Valetta and said, "You know, Mom, this is a great day for Dad, but a sad one for us."

SOMETHING TO THINK ABOUT

Why do you think that Henry decided to travel around the world, even though he was so sick?

_____

_____

_____

_____

ACTION PLAN

Read about OMS missionaries around the world on the One Mission Society website at www.onemissionsociety.org. What are some of the ministries they are involved in?

_____

_____

_____

_____

VERSE TO MEMORIZE

Those who are wise will shine as bright as the sky, and those who lead many to righteousness will shine like the stars forever. —Daniel 12:3

TALK TO GOD

Henry and Valetta Steel visited several countries and the OMS missionaries serving in those countries. Thank God for the impact their visit had and how it helped build the ministries in those countries. Ask Him to give the missionaries there today strength to focus on the work He has called them to do.

MY PERSONAL DIARY

_____

_____

_____

_____

_____

CHAPTER 9

FOLLOWING IN THEIR FATHER'S FOOTSTEPS

Lorna's excitement turned to devastation. She guided her mom discreetly into the kitchen. "Mom," she whispered, "I didn't know we were having a guest! I haven't cooked enough food! What am I going to do?"

Valetta took her 15-year–old daughter into a comforting embrace. "It's okay dear. There will be plenty of food to go around. I don't eat much." Lorna mustered fresh courage and began serving Indian curry and vegetables, a new dish for her brother to try. She wanted Leon and his friend, Don, to have enough food to satisfy their big appetites!

Lorna was so excited to have her big brother home. She missed him now that he was at college. Ever since their dad died, they had always had each other and had worked at their relationship. They were the best of friends.

After graduating from high school in December, Leon had moved to Greenville College in January, just three weeks earlier, to begin studies. He was energized by all the opportunities the college offered. Already, he had been asked to join a music group called *The Re-Created,* which would tour on weekends in churches, sharing Jesus. He was eager to see his mother and sister and tell them about his first few weeks at college. It was going to be a great weekend.

Mealtime was full of laughter. After dinner, Leon asked Valetta, "Hey, Mom, could Don and I go to the bowling alley for a few games? Then we'll come home and all relax together for the evening. And can Lorna come too?"

"That sounds like a wonderful idea, Leon." Valetta responded. "You kids get going, and I'll take care of the dishes."

Valetta smiled as her teenagers grabbed their coats and noisily headed out to the car. They were wonderful kids. She was so proud of them, yet they were so different from each other.

Valetta reflected on the live of her two precious children. Both Leon and Lorna had decided years earlier to let Jesus be the Lord of their lives. Lorna had questioned her mother one day, "Mommy, how can I know I am a Christian and that I will go to heaven when I die?"

Valetta was thrilled her little girl had come to her to ask such an important question. "Well, my dear, Jesus is waiting for you to accept His gift. He took your place and mine on the cross. If we accept what He has done for us, we can be friends with Him forever." Right then and there, at five years of age, Lorna prayed, "Dear Jesus, forgive me for the things I have done that make You sad. Please come into my heart."

God had been working in Leon's life as well, preparing him to make a decision to follow Jesus. One night, Valetta heard Leon crying in his bed. She ran into his room. "Mommy," he sobbed, "I just saw Jesus dying on the cross in my dreams."

Several weeks later, the family attended a service to hear Henry preach. Leon asked his parents if he could stay after the meeting and return home with his dad. When they arrived at home, Henry said to his wife, "This has been a very special night for me. Something exciting has happened. I had asked the Lord if I could lead my son to Him before I go to heaven. Tonight I did."

At seven years old, Leon made his own decision to know and love Jesus, totally separate from his family's choices to follow God.

Knowing that both of their children had made the decision to accept Jesus meant everything to Henry and Valetta. Their kids were a gift of God to them. But after Henry died, Valetta found parenting quite a challenge. Many times, she felt like a failure and wished her husband was there to be the father her children needed. She sometimes felt stressed and incapable of providing what they needed. She often felt sad and couldn't find the happiness she wanted to share with them each day.

One day, Leon confronted his mother, saying, "Mom, why do you always look so unhappy?" He was right. The sad things that had happened in her life had affected her greatly. She hadn't wanted either her baby Danny or her husband to die of cancer.

Valetta realized, though, that God had not taken away her happiness. She had let the toughness of life steal it away. "Lord," Valetta prayed, "please forgive me for thinking about myself and my problems so much. Please change me and help me live for You. And one more thing Lord … I totally let go of my ideas of what I think my life should be, and I ask You to give me Your ideas."

Asking forgiveness from God wasn't all that Valetta needed to do. She knew that her relationship with her kids was not as honest as it should be. She had to be humble and ask their forgiveness at times when she didn't act as she should. She found herself being more open with her teenagers. When she did something wrong, she said to them, "Leon, Lorna, I am sorry. I was wrong. Would you forgive me?" The children knew their mother's repentance was always genuine. They learned from Valetta's example how to ask for and receive forgiveness.

With more honesty and humility, their home was a much better place. The kids were more relaxed, everyone shared more, and Valetta, Leon and Lorna knew they were loved. They felt it not only from God but from each other.

Lorna was an outgoing girl who became everybody's friend. She was kind and loving and had a great relationship with her mother. Together, they cooked, sewed, raised dogs and told children about Jesus.

Leon enjoyed music and spent a lot of time playing his trombone and guitar. He and his sister used their musical gifts whenever an opportunity arose. They joined the church music group that played concerts for young people.

Leon was elected president of the church youth group and participated in the Bible quiz team. Once after hearing a stirring message from Ed Kilbourne, an OMS missionary to Korea, Leon said to his mom, "I think the Lord may be calling me to Korea as a youth worker." God was leading Leon in his father's footsteps.

Valetta was encouraged to hear from people outside the family about how her children were growing spiritually. Not only had she lost her husband, the children had lost their father as well. She knew they had to grieve also. But Valetta was thankful that their personal relationships with God helped them when they felt like giving up.

One of the young people from church approached Valetta one day and said, "Mrs. Steel, would you like to know what Leon said to us at our youth meeting last night?"

"Well, certainly," she replied, anxious to hear her son's thoughts.

"Leon told us, 'I miss my dad a lot, but I am finding that Jesus can be closer than a dad, and He's my best friend.'"

Valetta tried to blink back the tears. She could not have been more proud of her son. Yes, God had given her joy again, joy in spite of her sadness. Her teenagers were a gift from God to her. How thankful she was for their differences. Valetta brought her thoughts back to the pleasant dinner she had just shared with her kids and Leon's college friend.

The teenagers walked out into the cold and rainy weather. "Drive carefully," Valetta called as she waved to the carload of young people. She would be glad when their night of bowling was over and they were safe at home in the living room. They would drink hot chocolate and visit, catching up on school events, friends and church.

With the table cleared and dishes put away, Valetta gathered her papers to finish an article she had been writing. The doorbell interrupted her thoughts. Living in OMS housing at the World Headquarters was a blessing because coworkers and friends often dropped by unexpectedly for a chat or a cup of coffee. However, Valetta was startled as she opened the door. A cold breeze entered the house from the dark night.

"Are you Mrs. Steel?" the policeman hesitantly asked.

"Yes, I'm Mrs. Steel." *What was this about?* Valetta thought.

"Mrs. Steel, do you have a teenage boy, about 18, and a girl a little younger?"

"Yes, I do," Valetta slowly responded as she tightened her arms across her chest.

"Mrs. Steel, it's getting colder. The rain is turning to ice. There has just been an accident on Highway 37. I'm sorry to tell you that your children and their friend were killed in the accident."

Valetta froze. Her mind spun. This didn't make any sense. This wasn't real. The cold night air chilled her to the deepest part of her bones. She stepped back from the doorway. Suddenly, she felt the warm and comforting arms of her Savior hold her with a strength that surprised her.

"Officer, I know where they are," she heard herself say. "They are with God."

Valetta closed the door on the dark night. She couldn't believe what she had just heard. This couldn't be true. Had this really happened? Now, her whole family had been taken from her. All the people she loved the most in the world were gone. She knew it was not her fault that they had died. She was not to blame. Her head told her that God was not punishing her. He was a loving God, and He was in control. He could make good out of bad.

Valetta thought about the past few minutes that had changed her life totally. She fell to her knees and prayed to God, "God, you've taken baby Danny, my husband Henry and now my two precious teenage children, Lorna and Leon, to be with You. Be close to me now, and be everything I need in my sadness, which hurts so much."

God let Valetta peek into heaven. She saw that everything looked perfect, and she heard her children speak to her.

"Mother, won't you share our joy? Dad is here and our brother too. We're celebrating. Won't you celebrate with us?"

Valetta knew funeral arrangements had to be made. She'd done them before, but the last two times she had had some time to prepare. This time, death had happened so suddenly. She called a few of her friends, who went to her house and spent time with her, crying and talking. Then she thought about arranging the details of the funeral service. She felt sad but joyful. This funeral was going to be different.

She knew that some people would not understand how she could be happy after the death of her children, but Valetta knew they were with Jesus in heaven. She met with Pastor Don Riggs and told him, "You know, I think this was the best day of my children's lives, the day they saw Jesus. We should celebrate, even with our tears." Some of the kids from the youth group dropped by the house to let Valetta know how much they had loved her children. "We know that Lorna and Leon would like a funeral service that celebrates life, not death."

"Yes, that is how it will be, a celebration," Valetta said, and that is how it was.

SOMETHING TO THINK ABOUT
Why do you think God allowed Valetta to lose both Leon and Lorna in an accident after losing Danny and Henry years earlier?

_____

_____

_____

_____

ACTION PLAN
How would you like people to remember you after you die? Make up an announcement for a newspaper about how you lived your life and how you influenced people.

_____

_____

_____

_____

VERSE TO MEMORIZE
Even when I walk through the darkest valley, I will not be afraid, for you are close beside me. Your rod and staff protect and comfort me. — Psalm 23:4

TALK TO GOD
While we're on this earth, God wants us to concentrate on loving Him with all our hearts and loving others. But one day, we'll be with Him in heaven. Ask God to show you how to love others and tell them about Jesus so they, too, can go to heaven when they die.

MY PERSONAL DIARY

_____

_____

_____

_____

_____

CHAPTER 10

COFFEE AND MISSIONS

The strong smell of freshly brewed coffee drifted throughout the friendly chatter in the living room. Valetta had invited a group of friends and acquaintances over for a specific purpose. Her passion was to tell people about Jesus and help them understand more about missionaries and their work. Valetta would often say to her friends, "When we realize that we can know Jesus personally and He can solve our problems, we want the whole world to know Him too! I want to tell everyone about how to give their lives to Christ."

It wasn't easy to have the courage to invite all those people to her home, especially the ones she didn't know well. But after her husband died, Valetta practiced doing more things that she used to be afraid to do. Because her husband had been so competent, she often stayed in the background and quietly served in simple ways. Now life was different. She was doing things she never dreamed she would do.

❖ ❖ ❖

This wasn't the first time she had invited people to her home. She thought back to her first meeting, when Leon and Lorna were still alive. A smile spread across her face as she remembered the funny incident that sent the whole room into peals of laughter.

Valetta had invited a group of people to her home for coffee and a talk. She asked Leon if he would set up 30 folding chairs that were stored in one of the OMS buildings.

"Good grief, Mom! You want 30 chairs?" Leon protested as he flopped onto the sofa.

"You'll never get 30 people in here!"

"Maybe not," Valetta answered, "but I still want 30 chairs here in case we need them."

Twenty-five people arrived that evening. They sat on dining room chairs, the piano bench and the folding chairs Leon had set up. Five people sunk cozily into the soft sofa. When everyone had settled, the guest missionary began to speak. The room was quiet. The speaker was Valetta's brother-in-law, Dr. Virgil Ullom. He talked about God calling him from dental school to serve in Haiti. Everyone listened intently.

All of a sudden, a loud cracking sound interrupted the meeting. Five bodies fell into a heap as the leg of the old sofa broke. Silence filled the room, until someone let a stifled giggle escape. Then another muffled laugh couldn't be restrained. Soon, all 25 visitors were roaring with laughter. Leon couldn't contain himself. He thought it was the funniest thing that could have happened in a serious missionary meeting.

Yes, those had been good days. But now that her whole family was with God, Valetta put her energy into serving Him in any way she could. She started having coffee meetings again, and inviting people the Lord brought across her path. Soon people who didn't know Jesus were hearing how to become a Christian and giving their lives to Him.

Over the next several years, Valetta traveled to churches all around the United States. She encouraged church families to use home meetings to share the Gospel of Jesus Christ with friends and neighbors. Valetta continued in this effective ministry until the Lord called her to ministry in a new place.

In 1983, Valetta traveled to Taiwan on a short-term mission trip. The last time she had visited there was with her husband, 20 years earlier, just before he entered eternity. She had met and entertained many missionaries over the years. Now she would need to learn first-hand about living in a different country. She would learn about how people did things differently, spoke differently and believed differently.

That two-month trip turned into almost 10 years! Valetta fell in love with the Taiwanese people and their land of exotic markets, towering apartment buildings, luscious mountains and water-saturated rice paddies. She couldn't speak their language, but she could teach English and, at the same time, teach them about the God she served and what His Son did by dying on the cross.

God helped Valetta in her new country. She did what was familiar to her. She invited people into her home for tea and listened to them as they shared about what was making them sad. Valetta would then offer them Jesus.

She taught them how the Bible answered their many questions. They asked Valetta questions like, "What is the Bible about? Who is Jesus Christ?" and "Why wasn't Jesus Chinese?"

Bonnie Tsai was one of Valetta's helpers. She knew how to speak English and Chinese. So when Valetta taught her Bible studies in English, Bonnie interpreted them into Chinese. Bonnie's parents had worshiped idols all their lives. When they heard about Jesus, after much prayer from the Christians, Bonnie's parents confessed that Jesus was the Son of God.

Another of Valetta's helpers, Pauline Chen, told her some bittersweet news. Her parents told her never to come home again after she decided to follow Christ. Being a Christian in Taiwan was a serious decision. After some time, Pauline's parents changed their minds and let her live at home again. That was a miracle.

The spaces in Valetta's heart had previously been filled with her family; now they were filling up with new friendships and the thrill of leading people to Christ. She taught several English classes to the Chinese students.

One evening, while she was preparing dinner in her kitchen, she was surprised by a stranger. He had entered her home and was hiding so he could attack her. He turned the lights off and grabbed her, hurting her badly and touching her in places he shouldn't. She was afraid. When she cried out for help, the man ran away.

Valetta wondered why God had let such a bad thing happen, when she had already been through so many sad experiences. Judy Lee, one of Valetta's Taiwanese interpreters said to her, "Valetta, did you know that many of the students in your English classes and Bible studies have had bad things done to them as well? They are full of anger and unforgiveness." Valetta listened. "Maybe God wants you to understand these women better. Maybe He wants you to help them learn to forgive and be free on the inside. God can take away the anger and hurt that ties them up in knots."

Valetta knew once again that God really was in charge of her life. She could trust Him to care for her in every way.

SOMETHING TO THINK ABOUT

Even after all of Valetta's bad experiences, she still loved Jesus and wanted to serve Him. Do you always want to serve Him, even when things go wrong?

_____

_____

_____

_____

ACTION PLAN

Write a letter to God, telling Him about the unkind things people may have done to hurt you. Ask God to help you forgive the people so that the chains that tie you up in sadness will be broken. Get an adult you trust to help you burn the letter. Ask God to comfort your heart, and commit to loving Him no matter what happens in your life.

_____

_____

_____

_____

VERSE TO MEMORIZE

God blesses those who patiently endure testing and temptation. Afterward they will receive the crown of life that God has promised to those who love him. —James 1:12

TALK TO GOD

Ask God to help you forgive people who have hurt you. Pray also that He will help you trust Him completely. Praise Him for turning those hurts into something good.

MY PERSONAL DIARY

_____

_____

_____

_____

_____

CHAPTER 11

GOD'S BIG SURPRISE

In 1994, God's path led Valetta back to the OMS World Headquarters in Greenwood, Indiana. One day, some of her OMS friends approached her.

"Valetta," Juanita said, "why don't you come with Ruth, Arlene and me? We walk early each morning in the Greenwood Mall for exercise, before the shops open."

"That would be perfect!" Valetta said. "I need to get used to this country again, and being with you girls will do the trick!"

One morning, as Valetta was leaving the mall after walking, a man's voice interrupted her thoughts. "Do you remember me?" he asked.

Valetta thought quickly and tried to place when they had met. "Yes, Al Crumley," she recalled. "You came to visit the OMS office back in 1972 after your wife died of cancer and just after my children died. I gave you a tour and told you that OMS needed doctors."

"Yes," he said.

Valetta and Al understood each others' pain. They had both experienced sadness in losing the ones they loved. "Do you think we could have Chinese food and chat?" he suggested.

After their meal, they realized that they had a lot in common. They both grew up in homes that believed Jesus is the Son of God and that He died for their sins. They both loved Him and served Him. Dr. Al, a hospital administrator and pharmaceutical specialist, was about to go on his fifth short-term mission trip to World Gospel Mission's hospital in Kenya, Africa. Valetta and Al enjoyed travel, photography and being with friends.

One date turned into more meals together, meeting the family, an engagement and, eventually, a wedding. On September 24, 1994, Dr. Al and Valetta were married. Together, they have traveled to serve missionaries in many countries. In Africa, Dr. Al looked after sick people in the hospital. Dr. Al and Valetta also went on a safari. In East Asia, they met pastors who were in prison because they preached the Gospel. In other countries, they told people in churches, homes and Bible colleges about Jesus.

Valetta boasts that God has given her a wonderful gift in Al. Al is her personal doctor, chauffeur, companion and prayer partner. God filled the empty places in their hearts when He gave them to each other.

Dr. Al and Valetta feel that, just like Job in the Bible, the end of their lives is better than the beginning. Valetta lost all of her own children, but now, God has given her children and grandchildren through her marriage to Dr. Al!

Valetta's name is Italian for "valley." Her journey through life has taken her through many valleys. But she kept following Jesus, and He led her to the mountains where she could look back and see how He had carried her along His paths for her.

The Christian life is a great adventure. God is always up to something wonderful in our lives. Even though His adventure may take us through difficult valleys, He will never leave us. If we follow His path, we will be able to see that He leads us up the mountains as well. We can look back and see how He was with us and look ahead and see His good plans for the future. His love never fails.

SOMETHING TO THINK ABOUT

What is the difference between what you need and what you want? How has God provided you with all that you need?

_____

_____

_____

_____

ACTION PLAN

Think of someone you know who is going through a difficult time. Pray for God to help him through the valley, and make a card to encourage him.

_____

_____

_____

_____

VERSE TO MEMORIZE

God is able to do far more than we could ever ask for or imagine. He does everything by his power that is working in us. Give him glory in the church and in Christ Jesus. Give him glory through all time and for ever and ever. Amen. Ephesians 3:20-21 (NIrV)

TALK TO GOD

Sometimes, when we are in a difficult situation, it is hard to find the good in it. Ask God to give you His eyes to see the good He is doing around you. Thank Him for the surprises that He gives us.

MY PERSONAL DIARY

_____

_____

_____

_____

_____